Dolphin
Dive

James
Buckley, Jr.

SCHOLASTIC

New York Toronto Lo̶n̶
Sydney Mexico City New

Read more! Do more!

After you read this book, download your free all-new digital activities.

You can show what a great reader you are!

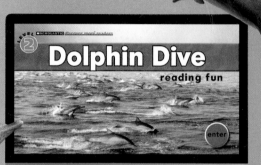

For Mac and PC

Take quizzes about the fun facts in this book!

Play dolphin games and do activities with videos and sounds!

Log on to

www.scholastic.com/discovermore/readers

Enter this special code: **L24PMRCRXFP2**

Contents

Copyright © 2014 by Scholastic Inc.

All rights reserved. Published by Scholastic Inc., *Publishers since 1920*.
SCHOLASTIC, SCHOLASTIC DISCOVER MORE™, and associated logos are trademarks
and/or registered trademarks of Scholastic Inc.

No part of this publication may be reproduced, stored in a retrieval system,
or transmitted in any form or by any means, electronic, mechanical, photocopying,
recording, or otherwise, without written permission of the publisher.
For information regarding permission, write to Scholastic Inc.,
Attention: Permissions Department, 557 Broadway, New York, NY 10012.

ISBN 978-0-545-63632-2

12 11 10 9 8 7 6 5 4 3 2 1   14 15 16 17 18 19/0

Printed in the U.S.A.   40
This edition first printing, April 2014

Scholastic is constantly working to lessen the environmental
impact of our manufacturing processes. To view our
industry-leading paper procurement policy,
visit www.scholastic.com/paperpolicy.

Ocean acrobats

Here come the acrobats of our seas! With flicks of their tails, dolphins leap high into the air.

NEW WORD

porpoise
POR-puhs
The dolphins are **porpoising** to go even faster.

SAY IT OUT LOUD

It's a fact!

Dolphins can leap as high as 20 feet

Dolphins love to show off for one another. They may even do somersaults! Watch them porpoising, or jumping in arches. They race across the water.

Porpoising

Somersaulting

out of the water. That's high!

Have you seen a bottlenose dolphin doing flips? There are 42 kinds of dolphin. Most are between 5 and 8 feet long. The orca is the biggest. It can be the size of a school bus!

Bottlenose dolphin

Orca

Dusky dolphin

Spotted dolphins

Humpbacked dolphin

There are a few kinds of dolphin that live in freshwater rivers. They have long beaks. The Amazon River dolphin can be pink!

White-sided dolphin

Spinner dolphins

Amazon River dolphin

All around a dolphin

This giant orca swims onto the beach. Then it grabs a seal!

Dolphins look like fish, but they are actually mammals. Dolphins cannot breathe underwater. They breathe air, like we do. Like other mammals, dolphins give birth to live young. The mother produces milk to feed her babies.

NEW WORD

mammal
MAM-uhl
Humans, dogs, cows, and dolphins are all **mammals**.

SAY IT OUT LOUD

SEA MAMMALS

Walrus

Sea lion

Whale

Otter

Seal

9

Dolphins are the fastest mammals that live in water. A dolphin's body is perfect for speedy swimming. Water moves easily over its smooth skin. Strong muscles in its tail push the dolphin through the water. Its fins help it steer, spin, and flip.

A dolphin breathes through a blowhole.

The dolphin's beak helps cut through the water.

Who's the fastest?

Mackerel: 2 mph

Fastest human swimmer (mammal): 5.5 mph

The dorsal fin helps keep the dolphin from rolling over.

The tail flaps up and down to move the dolphin along.

The flippers help the dolphin steer.

Dolphin (mammal): 20–40 mph

Great white shark: 25–35 mph

Sailfish: 67 mph

Dolphins together

Dolphins are not often alone. They live in big groups called pods. Pods have 15–20 members. The dolphins look out for one another. They hunt and take care of babies together.

It's a fact!

Dolphin pods sometimes join together to

NAMES OF ANIMAL GROUPS

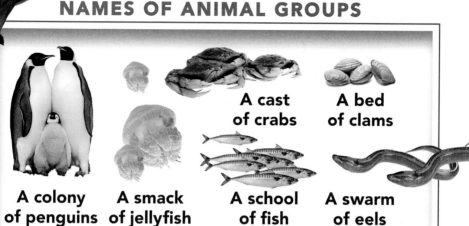

A colony
of penguins

A smack
of jellyfish

A cast
of crabs

A school
of fish

A bed
of clams

A swarm
of eels

form superpods of up to 1,000 dolphins!

When a female gives birth to a baby dolphin, called a calf, other pod members help her. They may even babysit! Female dolphins have one calf at a time.

Mom teaches her baby how to hunt and protect itself.

The mother helps her baby to the surface for its first breath. The calf drinks its mother's milk for about 18 months. Mom and baby stay close to each other for at least 5 years. They might even stay in the same pod for life.

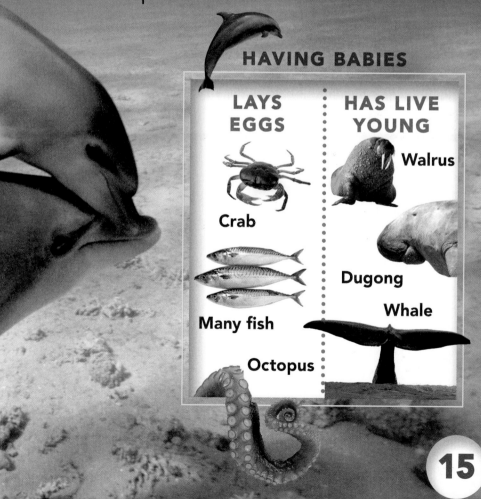

HAVING BABIES

LAYS EGGS	HAS LIVE YOUNG
Crab	Walrus
Many fish	Dugong
Octopus	Whale

The best thing about living in a pod is playing together! Sometimes dolphins chase one another. They even seem to play a game like tag!

Dolphins blow bubble rings at one another.

This dolphin is playing with a leaf!

Some dolphins are shy. Some are great big show-offs! They flip seaweed to one another. They balance things on their beaks. Dolphins even play with bubbles.

Dolphins touch one another to say "HI!"

Dolphins know who their best friends are.

Dolphins love to chase one another.

prey
pray
Dolphins hunt for **prey** to eat.

18

Time to eat!

Mackerel

A hungry dolphin searches for food. It is looking for fish, squid, or a tasty octopus. The dolphin uses its sharp eyes to find prey. It spots a fish and races after it. The dolphin grabs the fish. Its small, pointed teeth easily grip the slippery fish. Within seconds, the dolphin has swallowed it whole.

Squid

Dolphins don't chew with their teeth. They just use them to grab prey.

Tarpon

Shrimp

19

Dolphins don't use only sight to find food. They hunt using sound, too. A dolphin makes clicking noises. The sounds move through the water and hit fish or other prey.

The sounds come back to the dolphin as echoes. Then the dolphin knows where its next meal is!

These animals also hunt with echoes.

Dolphins can click hundreds of times each second.

Bat (mammal)

Shrew (mammal)

Swiftlet (bird)

21

Dolphins hunt best when they are together! A group of dolphins finds a school of fish. The dolphins surround the school. They swim in a big circle. The dolphins herd the fish to the center. The school becomes a tight ball. The dolphins take turns diving in to grab fish. That's teamwork!

These birds join
in on the feast.

herd
hurd
Shepherds **herd**
flocks of sheep.

Dolphin smarts

Dolphins are supersmart animals. They use their brains to hunt and stay safe. They even use tools. Dolphins near Australia put sea sponges on their beaks. This protects them when they dig for fish in sand! Dolphins also talk to one another. Each dolphin has its own sound, almost like a name.

Charles Potter, from the National Museum of Natural History, says:

"We don't know if dolphins have names exactly like humans do. We do know that they identify themselves with their own whistles. Each one has its own call."

This dolphin is carrying seaweed in its mouth.

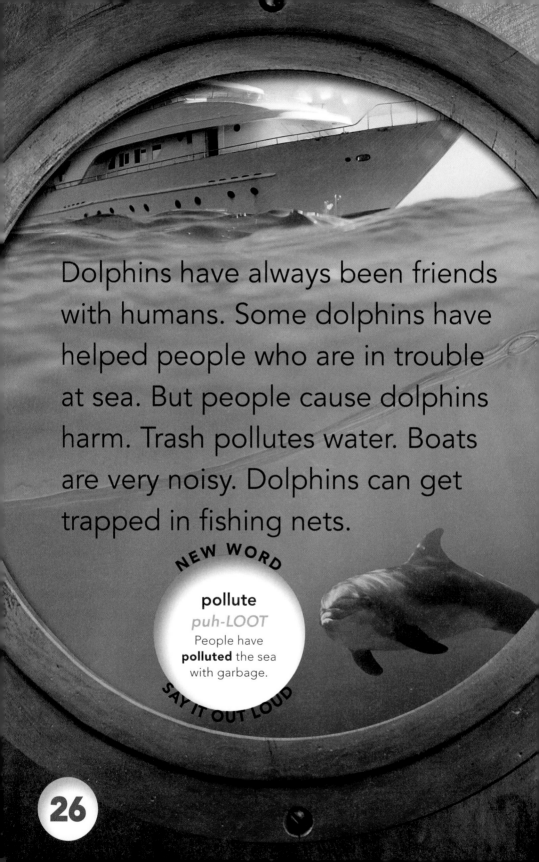

Dolphins have always been friends with humans. Some dolphins have helped people who are in trouble at sea. But people cause dolphins harm. Trash pollutes water. Boats are very noisy. Dolphins can get trapped in fishing nets.

NEW WORD

pollute
puh-LOOT
People have **polluted** the sea with garbage.

SAY IT OUT LOUD

In 2007, a surfer was attacked by a great white shark. A dolphin pod saved his life!

In 2008, a dolphin called Moko rescued two whales that were stranded.

In the 1960s, a dolphin named Flipper starred in his very own TV show!

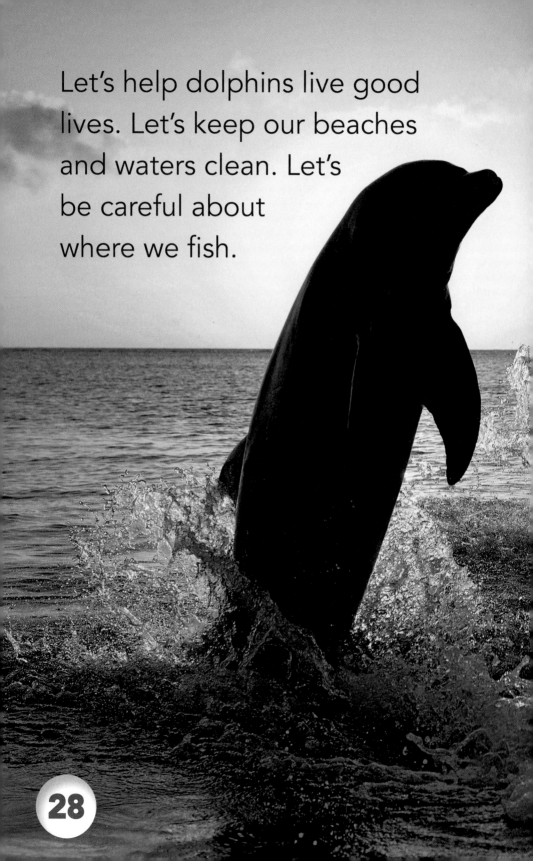

Let's help dolphins live good lives. Let's keep our beaches and waters clean. Let's be careful about where we fish.

These beautiful animals need our help to go on leaping through our seas. Their future depends on us.

Glossary

acrobat
A person or animal that does physical tricks.

beak
The pointy jaw on a dolphin.

blowhole
The opening in the top of a dolphin's head that lets it breathe.

calf
The young of a dolphin.

dorsal fin
The flat body part on a dolphin's back.

echo
A sound that bounces back from an object.

flipper
A flat body part that a dolphin uses to swim.

freshwater
Water that is not salty.

herd
To move animals together in a group.

mammal
A warm-blooded animal. Mammals breathe air and feed milk to their young.

muscle
Body tissue that pulls on bones to make them move.

Have you ever seen a dolphin leap and play?

pod
A group of dolphins. Two or more pods can join to make a very large superpod.

pollute
To make dirty.

porpoise
To travel through water by making short leaps into the air.

prey
An animal that is hunted by another animal as food.

school
A group of fish that swim together.

sea sponge
A soft sea animal with many holes.

squid
A sea animal with a long, soft body and ten arms.

stranded
Left or stuck in a strange place.

Index

Images
Alamy Images: 27 b (AF archive), 18 main (Cornforth Images), 16 l (Fco. Javier Gutiérrez/age fotostock), 12 b bg, 13 b (George Karbus Photography/Cultura RM), 1 (IS2008-11/Image Source), 14, 15 bg (Jeff Rotman), 28, 29 (Radius Images), 8, 9 bg (WILDLIFE GmbH); Dreamstime: cover silhouettes (Bluedarkat), cover sea (Dundanim), cover splash (Emevil), 25 t (Mvogel); FLPA: 27 c; Fotolia/Andriy Bezuglov: 21 c; Getty Images: 16 r (Eco/UIG), 18 mackarel (Frank Greenaway), cover r dolphin (Stephen Frink), 25 b (Wild Horizon/ Universal Images Group); iStockphoto: 6 br (ad_doward), 10 br (albertc111), 13 cr (AlexRaths), 11 cl (alexxx1981), 21 shrew silhouette, 21 swift silhouette (Andrew_Howe), 21 shrimp (antos777), 11 cr, 32 t (Becart), 19 b (bennyartist), 11 br (Big_Ryan), 2 t, 9 t, 13 tl, 15 dolphin (crookedart), 5 t (DavidMSchrader), 15 crab (dial-a-view), 4 inset, 12 b inset (dondesigns), 20 tc, 21 blue fish (dsafanda), 25 paper (Electric_Crayon), 25 l (Floortje), 5 b (FourOaks), 13 cl (German), 9 cr, 20 b (GlobalP), 13 tc (HQPhotos), 6 tr (jandaly), 20 tl, 21 yellow fish (marcatkins), 20 bg reef and octopus, 21 bg reef (Mark_Doh), 13 tr (MarkGillow), inside front cover (matsiash), 13 cfl (Mint_ Images), 10 t, 10 c (Musat), 6 bg, 7 bg (Nastco), 27 t (Peter_Nile), 15 fish (PicturePartners), 20 bat silhouettes, 21 bat silhouettes (pixitive), 21 picasso fish (richcarey), 3 bg, 18 bg water, 19 bg, 20 bg sea, 21 bg sea (Rike_), 9 br (RodKaye), 16 bubbles (RoyalSpirit), 11 t (RuslanDashinsky), 2 computer (skodonnell), tape throughout (spxChrome), 2 c, 7 tl (tswinner), 9 bl (wellesenterprises), 9 cl (zanskar); Nature Picture Library/Brandon Cole: cover l dolphin; Scholastic, Inc.: 11 bl; Science Source: 21 t (Art Wolfe), 16 b, 17 b, 22, 23, 32 b (Christopher Swann); Shutterstock, Inc.: 2 b, 7 c (Anna segeren), 10 bc (Bokica), 17 l (Croisy), 18 bg fish, 19 c (DJ Mattaar), 26 bg, 27 bg (Eky Studio), 24 r (Elena Larina), 10 bl (Koshevnyk), 10 bg, 11 bg (Matt9122), 15 dugong (mrHanson), 30, 31 (niall dunne), 15 tail (olon), 3 inset, 6 l (Ricardo Canino), 21 crab (RRomachkina), 19 tl (RWBrooks), 15 tentacle (Stasis Photo), 24 l (Steve Noakes), 19 tr (trevor brown), 13 cfr (vanchai), 17 r, 26 main (Willyam Bradberry); Thinkstock: 15 walrus (Fuse), back cover (Jami Garrison).

Science Source: 21 t (Art Wolfe), 16 b, 17 b, 22, 23, 32 b (Christopher Swann); 7 bl (Dr. Carleton Ray), 4 bg, 5 bg (F. Stuart Westmorland), 7 br (Jerry L. Ferrara), 7 tr (Terry Whittaker);